Symphony No. 3
in D Minor
for Alto Solo, Choirs and Orchestra

Gustav Mahler

DOVER PUBLICATIONS, INC.
Mineola, New York

Bibliographical Note

This Dover edition, first published in 2002, is a republication of the edition originally published by Universal Edition, Vienna, n.d. [1906]. Lists of contents and instrumentation, poetic texts, glossary, and all footnote translations in the score are newly added.

International Standard Book Number

ISBN-13: 978-0-486-42138-4
ISBN-10: 0-486-42138-4

Manufactured in the United States by LSC Communications
42138406   2016
www.doverpublications.com

CONTENTS

Symphony No. 3
in D Minor

for Alto Solo, Women's Chorus,
Boys' Chorus, and Orchestra

Composed 1893-96 / revised 1906

First complete performance:
Krefeld, Germany / 9 June 1902

Texts & Translations   vi
Instrumentation   vii
Glossary   viii

1. Abtheilung
[Part 1]

I. Kraftig. Entschieden • *Robustly. Resolute*   1

2. Abtheilung
[Part 2]

II. Tempo di Menuetto. Grazioso   103

III. Comodo. Scherzando. Ohne Hast *(Without haste)*   132

IV. "O Mensch! Gib Acht!" • *"O man! Attend!"*   179
Text from Nietzsche: *Also sprach Zarathustra*

V. "Es sungen drei Engel" • *"Three angels were singing"*   190
Text from *Des Knaben Wunderhorn*

VI. Langsam. Ruhevoll. Empfunden • *Slow. Peaceful. Deeply felt*   208

Texts and Translations

O Mensch! Gib Acht!
Was spricht die tiefe Mitternacht?
Ich schlief!
Aus tiefem Traum bin ich erwacht!
Die Welt ist tief!
und tiefer als der Tag gedacht!
O Mensch! Tief, tief ist ihr Weh!
Lust tiefer noch als Herzeleid!
Weh spricht: Vergeh!
Doch alle Lust will Ewigkeit!
will tiefe, tiefe Ewigkeit.

O man! Attend!
What says the deep midnight?
I slept!
From a deep dream have I awoken!
The world is deep!
and deeper than the day has imagined!
O man! Deep, deep is its suffering!
Joy deeper still than heart's sorrow!
Suffering speaks: Perish!
But all joy desires eternity!
desires deep, deep eternity.

From Nietzsche, *Also sprach Zarathustra*

ARMER KINDER BETTLERLIED

Es sungen drei Engel einen süssen Gesang;
mit Freuden es selig in dem Himmel klang,
sie jauchzten fröhlich auch dabei,
dass Petrus sei von Sünden frei,
er sei von Sünden frei.
Und als der Herr Jesus zu Tische sass,
mit seinen zwölf Jüngern das Abendmahl ass:
Da sprach der Herr Jesus: Was stehst du denn hier?
Wenn ich dich anseh', so weinest du mir!
Und sollt' ich nicht weinen, du gütiger Gott.
(Du sollst ja nicht weinen! Sollst ja nicht weinen!)
Ich hab' übertreten die zehn Gebot.
Ich gehe und weine ja bitterlich.
Ach komm und erbarme dich über mich!
Hast du denn übertreten die zehen Gebot,
so fall auf die Kniee und bete zu Gott!
Liebe nur Gott in alle Zeit!
So wirst du erlangen die himmlische Freud',
die himmlische Freud', die selige Stadt,
die himmlische Freude war Petro bereit't,
durch Jesum und allen zur Seligkeit.

POOR CHILDREN'S BEGGING SONG

Three angels were singing a sweet song;
with joy it resounded blissfully in heaven,
they rejoiced also
that Peter was free from sin,
he was free from sin.
And when the Lord Jesus sat at table,
with his twelve disciples ate the supper,
There spoke the Lord Jesus: What are you doing?
Whenever I look at you, I find you weeping!
And should I not weep, you gracious God.
(You should truly not weep! Should truly not weep!)
I have broken the Ten Commandments.
I go and weep most bitterly.
Ah, come and have mercy on me!
If you have broken the Ten Commandments,
then fall on your knees and pray to God!
Only love God forever!
Thus will you attain heavenly joy,
heavenly joy, the holy city,
heavenly joy was prepared for Peter
by Jesus and for all for their salvation.

From *Des Knaben Wunderhorn*

SYMPHONY NO. 3

Instrumentation

4 Flutes [Fl.]
  (Fl. 3,4 = Piccolos [Picc.] 1,2)[1]
4 Oboes [Ob.]
  (Ob. 4 = English Horn [Engl. Horn, Englhr.])
3 Clarinets (B♭,A) [Clarinette, Cl. (B,A)][2]
  (Cl. 3 = Bass Clarinet (B♭) [Bassclarinette, Basscl. (B)])
2 E♭ Clarinets [Clarinette in Es, Cl. in Es][3]
  (E♭ Cl. 2 = Cl. 4)
4 Bassoons [Fagott, Fag.]
  (Bsn. 4 = Contrabassoon [Contrafagott, Ctrfag.])
8 Horns (F)
4 Trumpets (F,B♭) [Trompete, Trmp. (F,B)][4]
4 Trombones [Posaune, Pos.]
Contrabass Tuba [Contra-Bass Tuba, Tuba, Btb.]
2 Timpani [Pauke, Pk.], 3 drums each
2 Glockenspiels [Glockensp., Glcksp.], sounding an octave higher than notated
Tambourine [Tambr.]
Tam-tam
Triangle [Triangel, Trgl.]
Suspended Cymbal [Becken (freihängend), Beck. (frei)], to be reinforced by a second Cymbal
Side Drum [Kleine Trommel, Kl. Tr.]
Bass Drum [Grosse Trommel, Gr. Tr.]
Cymbal [Becken, Beck.], attached to the Bass Drum and struck with the drum by the same player
Switch [Ruthe], for striking the wood of the Bass Drum
2 Harps [Harfe]
Violins I, II [Violine, Viol.][5]
Violas
Cellos [Violoncell, Vcl.]
Basses [Contrabass, Cb.], some with low C-strings

Alto solo
Women's Choir [Frauenchor]

In the distance [in der Ferne (Entfernung) aufgestellt]:
  Flugelhorn (B♭) [Flügelh. (B)]
  Several Side Drums [kleine Trommeln]

In a high gallery [in der Höhe postiert]:
  4 (if possible, 5 or 6) tuned Bells [abgestimmte Glocken, Glocken]
  Boys' Choir [Knabenchor]

The symphony is divided into two parts. Part 1 consists of movement I, Part 2 of movements II, III, IV, V, and VI. After Part 1 a long pause.

Note: All trills are to be performed without final turns [Nachschläge], even where this is not explicitly stated.

---

[1] At two points (1st and 5th movements), 4 piccolos are used (in place of 4 flutes).
[2] Cl. 1 doubled if possible.
[3] Reinforced if possible in 5th movement.
[4] 2 more high trumpets to be used for reinforcing if possible. E♭ Cornet to be substituted for Tpt. 1 at one point in 1st movement if possible.
[5] Very large complements of all strings.

Glossary

(The words appear here exactly as they appear in the score.)

ab, off
abdämpfen, damp
aber, but
abnehmend, waning
abreissen, break off, flag
alle(s), all
allmählich, gradually
als, like, than
alten, old
am, at the
an, to
andern, others
Anfang(e), beginning
Anfangstempo, opening tempo
angebunden, played at the same time
Anmerkung, note
anmuthig, gracefully
anschwellend, crescendo
anzuschlagen, to be struck
As, A♭
auf, on, for
aufgehob., aufgeh., aufg., raised
aufgestellt, placed
aus, from
(sich) ausbreitend, broadening out
Ausdruck, expression
ausdrucksvoll, expressively
ausgeführt, played
auszuhalten, to sustain
B, B♭
Bässe, double basses
bedächtig, deliberate
befestigt, attached
beginnen, begin
behaglich, comfortable
bei, on
beide, both
beinahe, almost
besonders, especially
Betonungen, accentuation
bewegt, animated, agitated
bewegter, più mosso
Bewegung, motion, tempo
bezeichneten, marked
bis zum, until the
bitterlich, bitterly
bleiben, remain, *bleibt*, remains
Bogen, bow
brechen, arpeggiate
breit, broad, broadly, *breiter*, more broadly
Celli, cellos

Cis, C♯
Consonanten, consonant
Dämpfer, mute, mutes, muting
das, the
dasselbe, the same
dem, den, the
der, the, of the, who
Des, D♭
deutlich, clearly
die, the
diesen, this
Dirigenten, conductor
dirigiren, conduct, beat
doch, but
Doppelgriff, Dopplgr., double stop
drängend, pressing, *drängender*, more pressing
dumpf, muffled, dull
durch, (obtained) through
durchaus, throughout
eben, just previously
ebenfalls, likewise
ebenso, just as
Echoton, echo tone
edlen, noble, exalted
eilen, hurry, *ohne zu .eilen*, without hurrying
eilend, hurrying
eine, einem, a, one (player)
einer, eines, of a
einige, several
(sich) entfernend, becoming distant
Entfernung, distance
Empfindung, feeling, emotion
empfunden, (deeply) felt
entschieden, resolute
erste(n), first
ersterbend, dying away
Es, E♭
etwas, somewhat
Ferne, distance
feurige, fiery
Fidel, medieval fiddle
Figuren, figures
Fis, F♯
Flag., harmonics
fliessend, flowing
folgend, following, in keeping with
fort, continuing
fortlaufend(er), running, continuous
frei, freely
freihängend, suspended
frisch, vigorous, lively
früher, earlier
für, for

furchtbarer, formidable
ganzes, full
ganzlich, completely
gebrochen, arpeggiated
gebunden, legato
gedämpft, damped
gedehnt, drawn out
gehalten(en), held, held back, meno mosso
gehaltener, more restrained
geheimnisvoll(er), mysterious
gehen, go
gemächlich, comodo, easily, *gemächlicher, più comodo*
gemässigt(e), moderate
geringste, briefest
gerissen, cut off
Ges, G♭
gesangvoll, cantabile
gesättigten, saturated
geschlagen, struck
gestimmt, tuned
gestopft, gest., stopped
gestrichen, bowed
gesungen, sung
getheilt, geth., divisi
getragen, solemn
Gewalt, power
gewirbelt, rolled
gewöhnlich(e), ordinario, normally
Gis, G♯
gleichen, equal-sized
gleichmässiger, even
grell, shrill
Gr. Fl., flute
Griffbrett, fingerboard, sul tasto
grob, coarsely, rudely
grossem, grosser, great, large
grössere, larger
gut, quite
H, B
Halbe, (beat in) half-notes
Hälfte, half (of a string section)
Halt, pause
hart, hard
Hast, haste
Haupttempo, principal tempo
Hauptzeitmass, principal tempo
herausgestossen, thrust out
hervortretend, hervortr., prominently
hier, here, *von hier an*, from here on
hinaufziehen, approaching from below
hinunterziehen, approaching from above
hoch, high

viii

höchster, greatest
hohe, high
Höhe, elevation, *in die Höhe, i. d. Höhe,* up, in the air
höher, higher
Holzbläser, woodwinds
Holzschlägeln, wooden mallets
hörbar, audible
im, in, in the
immer, always
ja, absolutely
kaum, barely
keck, bold
keine, no
klagend, lamenting
Klang, sound
kleine, small
klingen, ring
klingt, sounds
Kopfstimme, head voice
Kraft, Kraftentfaltung, power
kräftig, robustly
kurz(er), short
Lage, position
lange, long
langhallenden, long-resounding
langsam, slow, *langsamer,* slower
(sich) lassen, allow
lebhaft, lively
leidenschaftlich, passionately
leise, softly
letzten, previous
lustig, merry, merrily
Marsch, march
mehr, more
mehrfach besetzt, several to a part
merklich, noticeably
mit, with
mittlere, medium, middle
möglich, possible
möglichst, as . . . as possible
munter, cheerfully
Musiker, musician
nach, (retune) to
nachgeben, broaden
nachhorchend, listening
nachlassen, relax
Nachschlag, Nachschl., turn (at end of trill)
nachzuahmen, to imitate
(sich) nähernd, drawing nearer
Naturlaut, sound of nature
natürlich, ordinario
nehmen, take, change to
nicht, not, don't
nimmt, take, change to
noch, still
Note, notes
Notfall, necessity, *nur im Notfall zur,* only if necessary for
nur, only
offen, open, unstopped
ohne, without
Oktav(e), octave

Orchester, orchestra
Piston, cornet, *kleinem Piston,* small cornet in E♭
plötzlich, suddenly, *plözlichem,* sudden
Pralltriller, mordents
Pulte, desks, stands
recht, quite, very
Rhythmus, rhythm
roh(er), rough, crude
Rücksicht, regard
ruhevoll, peaceful
ruhig, calm
Saite, string
sanft, soft
Satz, movement
Schalltrichter, Schalltr., bells (of wind instruments)
Schlägeln, mallets
schlagen, beat, conduct
schleppen, drag
Schluss, end
schmetternd, blaring, resounding
schnell, fast, *schneller,* faster
Schwammschlägeln, sponge mallets
schwer, heavy
Schwung, energy
schwungvoll, energetically
sehr, very
selben, same
singend, singing
so . . . als, as . . . as
sofort, immediately
Sordinen, mutes
Spieler, players, *2. Spieler,* second group of 1st violins
spring. Bog., sautillé
stark, strongly, *stärker,* stronger, *stärker besetzt,* more players to a part
Steg, bridge
steigernd, intensifying
Steigerungen, increases
stetig, stets, steadily
Stimme, voice, group of 1st violins
Streicher, strings
streng, strictly
Strich, bowstroke, *Strich für Strich,* one bow per note, détaché
stürmen, rage, rush
summend, humming
Takt, beat, time
taktiren, tactiren, conduct, beat
Tellern, *mit Tellern,* clashed cymbals
Tempowechsel, change in tempo
Theilen, sections
tief(e), low, *tiefer,* lower
Ton, note, tone, sonority
Tönen, notes
Tonhöhe, register
Triangelschlägel, triangle beater
Triller, trill
Triolen, triplets
über, over, *über das ganze Orchester hinaus,* rising above the whole orchestra

Übergange, transition
übernimmt, takes, changes to
überraschend, surprisingly
übertönend, rising above, *alles übertönend,* louder than the rest of the orchestra
und, and
ungefähr, approximately
unmerklich, imperceptibly
Unterstützung, reinforcement, support
verändern, changing
verdoppelt, doubled
verhallend, becoming fainter
verklingend, dying away
Verlaufe, course
(sich) verlierend, dying away
Vermittlung, transition
verschwindend, disappearing
versehen, provided
versieht, plays
vibrirend, vibrating, with vibrato
viel, much, a lot of
Viertel, quarter-notes
Vokal, vowel
vollziehen, execute, *vollzieht sich,* to be executed
vom, by the
von, by
vorgetragen, played
vorhanden, (is) available
vorher, vorhin, before
Vorschläge, grace notes
vorwärts, pressing forward
wechseln, change
weich, soft, gently
Weise, tune, call
weiter, far, *weitester,* farthest
welche, which
wenig, little
wenn, if
werden, becoming
wie, as, as though
wieder, again
wild, unrestrained
womöglich, wo möglich, if possible
Worte, words
wuchtiger, more heavily, more vigorously
zart(e), gentle, gently, tenderly
Zeit, time
zögernd, hesitating
zu, to, in, at, *zu 2, 3, 4,* unisono
zuerst, at first
zufahrend, pressing, stringendo
zuletzt, just previously
zum, zur, to the
zurückhalten(d), meno mosso, *zurückhaltender,* more restrained
zurückkehren, return, *zurückkehrend,* returning
zwei, two
1., 2., 3., 4., 1st, 2nd, 3rd, 4th
2te, 3te, 4te, 2nd, 3rd, 4th
2(3,4) fach, in 2(3,4) parts

SYMPHONIE No. 3.

I. Abtheilung.

No. 1.

Kräftig. Entschieden.

1.2. Flöte.

3.4. Flöte. (1.2. Piccolo.)

1.2.3. Oboe.

4. Oboe. (engl. Horn.)

1.2. Clarinette in B.

3. Clarinette in B. (Bassel.)

1.2. Clarinette in Es.

1.2.3. Fagott.

4. Fagott. (Contrafag.)

1.2.3.4.5.6.7.8. Horn in F.

Kräftig. Entschieden.

1.2.3.4. Trompete in F.

1.2.3.4. Posaune.

Contra-Basstuba.

Glockenspiel. Kl. Trommel.

Triangel. Tambourin.

Becken (freihängend.) Tamtam.
Becken. an der gr. Trommel befestigt und vom selben Musiker geschlagen, der die Trommel versieht.
Gr. Trommel.

1.2. Pauke. — 1. in A, B, E hoch. — 2. in D tief, B, F hoch.

1.2. Harfe.

1. Violine. **Kräftig. Entschieden.**

2. Violine.

Viola.

Violoncell.

Contrabass.

Anmerkung für den Dirigenten: Das Anfangstempo ist im Ganzen und Grossen für das ganze Stück durchaus festzuhalten und trotz der jeweiligen Taktwechsel oder Modificationen strengste Continuität desselben durchzuführen.

Note for the conductor: The opening tempo is, for the most part, to be retained throughout the whole movement, and the strictest continuity of tempo is to be maintained in spite of momentary changes in beat or modifications.

1

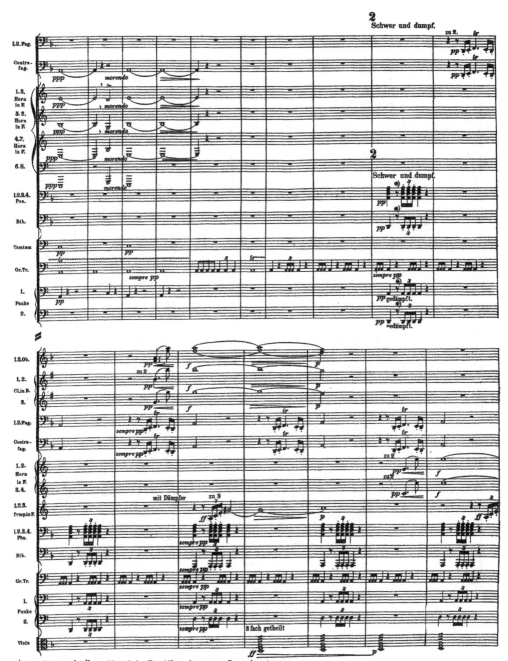

*) Diese Triolen schnell, ungefähr mit den Vorschlägen der grossen Trommel zusámmen.

*)These triplets *fast*, approximately simultaneously with those on the bass drum.

* Diese Triole immer. unter allen Umständen, schnell auszuführen!

*These triplets always, under all conditions, to be performed *fast!*

2. Stimme nur von den mit Contra-C versehenen Bässen.

* das A der I. Tr. ist <u>kein</u> **Druckfehler.**

*The A in the 1st Trumpet is *not* a typographical error.

1. 2. Fl.
1. 2. Picc.
1. 2. 3. 4. Ob.
1. 2. 3. Cl. in B.
1. 2. Cl. in Es.
1. 2. 3. Fag. Ctrfag.
1. 2. Horn in F.
3. 4. Horn in F.
5. 6. Horn in F.
7. 8.
1. 3. Trmp. in F.
2. 4.
1. 2. 3. Pos.
4. Tuba.
Trgl.
Gr. Tr.
1. Pk.
1. Viol.
2. Viol.
Viola.
Vcl.
Cb.
zu 2
zu 4
zu 3
poco a poco cresc.
1. 2. 3. Fag.
Dämpfer nehmen
sempre p
geth.
cresc.

+) *Anmerkung für den Dirigenten:* Diese Stelle muss von den Streichern mit höchster Kraftentfaltung gespielt werden, so dass die Saiten durch die heftige Vibration beinahe in Berührung mit dem Griffbrett gerathen. Der Wiener hat dafür den Ausdruck: „*schöppern*." Ein gleiches gilt von den Hörnern.

)Note for the conductor: This passage must be played by the strings with the greatest power, so that the individual strings, as a result of the violent vibration, almost come in contact with the fingerboard. The Viennese call this "schöppern." A similar effect applies to the horns.

Immer noch drängend.

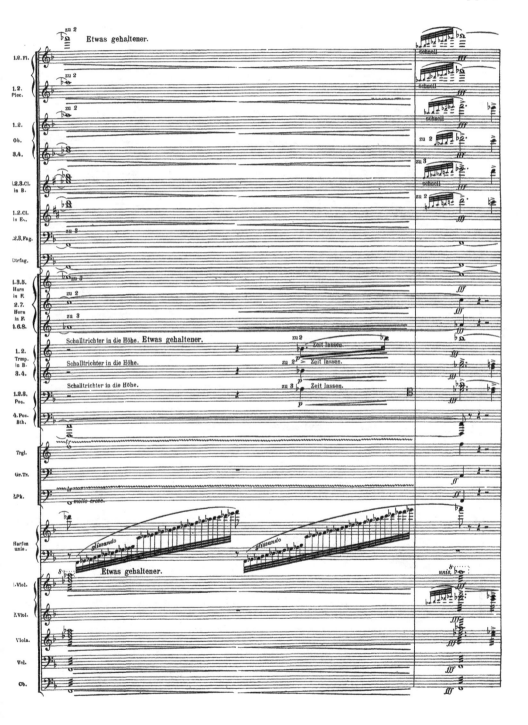

76
Mit höchster Kraft.
zu 2
dim.
scharf abreissen
1.2.Fl.
1.2. Picc.
1.2. Ob. 3.4.
1.2.3.Cl. in B.
1.2.Cl. in Es.
zu 3
1.2.3.Fag.
Ctrfag.
1.3.5.7. Horn. in F.
2. Horn. in F. 4.6.8.
zu 4
1.2. Trmp. in B. 3.4.
1.2.3. Pos.
4. Pos. Btb.
Kl-Tr.
Trgl.
cresc.
Tambr.
Beck.
Gr.Tr.
1. Pk. 2.
Harfen unis.
glisando
arco
1.Viol.
2.Viol.
Viola.
Vcl.
Cb.

Zweite Abtheilung.
N⁰ 2.

(Von * bis * kann das engl. Horn zuhilfe genommen werden, wenn der Oboist die Stelle nicht zart genug hervorbringen kann.)

(From * to * the English horn can be substituted if the oboist cannot perform the passage softly enough.)

L'istesso tempo.
(= wie früher =)
3
1.
Fl.
2.3.4.
p stacc.
stacc.
stacc.
1.2.
1.2.3.Ob.
pp
1.2.3.
zu 3
f
1.2.Cl. in B.
zu 2
zu 2
1.Cl. in Es.
p
1.2.Fag.
zu 2
f
L'istesso tempo.
Trgl.
p
1. Solo.
1. u. 2. unisono
1. 2. Harfe.
f nicht gebrochen
ff
spring. Bogen
Die ersten 4 Pulte.
1.Viol. geth.
3 fach geth.
f mit dem Bogen geschlagen
2 fach geth.
pizz.
2.Viol. geth.
f getheilt
Viola geth.
pizz.
Vcl.
Cb.

Sempre l'istesso tempo.
(= wie früher =)
9
1. Fl.
2.3. Fl.
2. Picc.
1. Ob. 2.3.
1.2.3. Cl. in B.
1.2.3. Fag.
1.2. Horn in F. 3.4.
1. Trmp. in F.
Harfen. unis.
1. Viol. 3 fach geth.
2. Viol. 3 fach geth.
Viola.
Vcl. geth.
Cb.
staccato
zu 2
zu 3
gestopft
mit Dämpfer
Doppelgriff
Doppelgriff.
pizz.
col legno
f col legno
f sempre col legno
spr. Bogen
spr. Bogen
arco
pp sempre
schnell
p mit dem Bogen geschlagen

10 Wieder etwas bewegter.
1.2. Fl.
3. Fl.
2. Picc.
1.2. Ob. 3.4.
1.2.3. Cl. in B.
1. Cl. in Es. 2.
1.2.3. Fag.
1.2. Horn in F. 3.4.
1. Trmp. in F. 2.3.
1. Harfe.
2. Harfe.
1. Viol. 3 fach geth.
2. Viol. 3 fach geth.
Viola geth.
Vcl. 3 fach geth.
Cb.
zu 2
zu 3
offen 1.
offen
mit Dämpfer
nicht brechen
pizz.
Doppelgriff.
arco
mit Dämpfer
spr. Bogen.
nicht geth.
geth.
gliss.

126 [II]

№ 3.

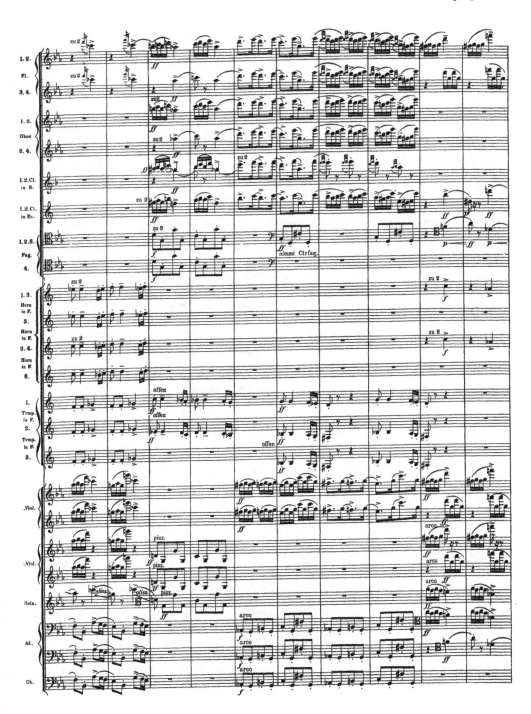

150 [III]

Anmerkung für den Dirigenten: ✱ ohne Rücksicht auf das Tempo.

Note for the conductor: *Fanfare—without regard for the tempo.

Anmerkung für den Dirigenten: Streicher ohne cresc.
Note for the conductor: No cresc. in the strings.

+) *Anmerkung für den Dirigenten.* Kein Irrthum! Mit dem Rücken des Bogens gestrichen!

Note for the conductor: Not an error! Bowed with the back of the bow!

1.2.Fl.
1.2.Picc.
1.2. Ob. 3.4.
1.2.3.Cl. in B.
1.2.Cl. in Es.
1.2. Fag. 3.4.
1.3. Horn in F. 2.5.4.6.
1.2. Trmp. in F. 3.
1.2. Pos. 3.
Btb.
Trgl.
Tambr. Beck. Tamtam
1.2. Pauke unis.
1.Viol. 8 fach geth.
2.Viol.
Viola
Vcl.
Cb.
zu 2
zu 3
cresc.
molto cresc.
pp cresc.
ohne Nachschl.
gest.
offen
mit Dämpfer
Tam-tam
Beck.
Tamb.
p molto cresc.
col legno
arco
geth.
col legno geschlagen
col legno geschl.
pp molto cresc.

Nᵒ. 4.

Worte von Nietzsche.

179

N.B. Zu dieser Stelle sind durchaus nur Bässe mit der tiefen Contra C-Saite zu benützen.

N.B. *Throughout* this passage *only basses* with *low C-strings* are to be used.

Folgt ohne Unterbrechung № 5.
No. 5 follows without interruption.

№ 5.

Worte aus des „Knaben Wunderhorn"

190

192 [V]

194 [V]

N̂. Diese 4 Takte werden geschlagen, wenn noch eine 5. Glocke in B vorhanden ist.
N.B. These four measures are to be played if a fifth bell in B♭ is available.

10
Glocken
Knabenchor
Je - sum und Al - len zur Se - lig - keit.
Bimm bamm bimm bamm
1.2.3.4. Picc.
zu 4
1. 2. Ob. 3.
zu 2
Engelhr.
1.2. Cl. in B. 3.
nimmt 2. Clar. in Es
Cl. in Es.
Basscl. in B.
1.2.3. Fag.
zu 3
Ctrfag.
1.3.5. Horn in F. 2.4.6.
1. 3.
4.6.
1. Trmp. in F. 2. Trmp. in F. 3.
offen
1.2. Pos.
Triangel
1. Harfe.
nicht brechen
2. Harfe.
Frauenchor.
Je - sum und Al - len zur Se - lig - keit.
Bimm bamm
Bimm bamm bimm bamm
Vcl.
durch Flag.
Cb

Folgt ohne Unterbrechung N⁰ 6.
No. 6 follows without interruption.

№ 6.

*) *Anmerkung für den Dirigenten:* Um die grösste Intensität des Tones zu erzielen, wechseln die Streicher möglichst oft, aber unmerklich, den Bogen.

Note for the conductor: In order to attain the greatest intensity of tone, the string players should change bows as often as possible, but inaudibly.

*) *Anmerkung für den Dirigenten*: Um die grösste Intensität des Tones zu erzielen, wechseln die Geiger möglichst oft, aber unmerklich, den Bogen.

*)*Note for the conductor:* In order to attain the greatest intensity of tone, the violins should change bows as often as possible, but inaudibly.

※ Tempoveränderungen ja nicht ruckweise.
*Change in tempo *must* not be done jerkily.

Nicht mit roher Kraft. Gesättigten, edlen Ton.
ohne Diminuendo. Nicht abreissen.
Lange
1. 2. Fl. 3. 4.
1. 2. Ob. 3. 4.
1. Cl. in B. 2. 3.
1. 2. Cl. in Es.
1. 2. 3. Fag.
Ctrfag.
1. 3. Horn in F.
2. 4. Horn in F.
5. 7. Horn in F.
6. 8.
1. 2. in F Trmp.
Trompeten über das ganze Orchester hinaus.
3. 4. in B.
1. 2. Pos. 3. 4.
Btb.
1. Pk. 2.
1. Viol.
2. Viol.
Viola
Vcl.
Cb.
zu 2
sempre p
sempre ff
2 f. geth.
3 f. geth.